PHYSICS
IN THE REAL WORLD

by Meg Marquardt

Content Consultant
David Jackson
Associate Professor, Science Education
University of Georgia

Core Library

An Imprint of Abdo Publishing
abdopublishing.com

abdopublishing.com

Published by Abdo Publishing, a division of ABDO, PO Box 398166, Minneapolis, Minnesota 55439. Copyright © 2016 by Abdo Consulting Group, Inc. International copyrights reserved in all countries. No part of this book may be reproduced in any form without written permission from the publisher. Core Library™ is a trademark and logo of Abdo Publishing.

Printed in the United States of America, North Mankato, Minnesota
082015
012016

Cover Photo: Greg Dale/National Geographic/SuperStock
Interior Photos: Greg Dale/National Geographic/SuperStock, 1; Masatoshi Okauchi/REX/
Newscom, 4; Red Line Editorial, 7, 40; Shutterstock Images, 8; iStockphoto, 10, 12, 15; Universal
History Archive/Getty Images, 16; Bettmann/Corbis, 18; AP Images, 20; Jan Woitas/Picture-
Alliance/DPA/AP Images, 22, 43; Martial Trezzini/Keystone/AP Images, 25; Unkel/ullstein bild/
Getty Images, 28; NASA, 30; BSIP/UIG/Getty Images, 32; Fairfax Media/Getty Images, 34;
Christian Petersen/Getty Images, 37, 45; Harold Cunningham/Getty Images, 38

Editor: Arnold Ringstad
Series Designer: Ryan Gale

Library of Congress Control Number: 2015945541

Cataloging-in-Publication Data
Marquardt, Meg.
 Physics in the real world / Meg Marquardt.
   p. cm. -- (STEM in the real world)
 ISBN 978-1-68078-042-0 (lib. bdg.)
 Includes bibliographical references and index.
 1. Physics--Juvenile literature.   I. Title.
 530--dc23
                                                                        2015945541

CONTENTS

CHAPTER ONE

DISAPPEARING ACT

In a laboratory, a physicist can make things disappear. He lines up four lenses. They are like those found in eyeglasses. But these lenses do not help a person see. Instead, they bend light around an object. This makes that object appear invisible. The physicist looks through the lenses. It seems as though the object is not there at all.

Physics makes incredible technologies, such as invisibility, possible.

Professor John Howell and graduate student Joseph Choi developed this method of invisibility. They did their research at the University of Rochester in New York. The device cost them just $1,000, and they believe it can be made even more cheaply.

Invisibility has long been a dream of science fiction writers. Physicists are making those dreams come true. Invisibility could have many uses. The military could use it to hide troops. It could also help in fields such as medicine. A surgeon

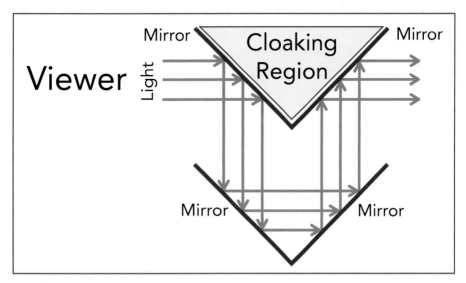

Invisibility Technology
This diagram shows how one simple method of invisibility
works. How does this help you better understand the
cloaking technology? What other uses can you think of for
invisibility?

could see right through her hands into a patient's
body.

    However, this technology is difficult to use. It is
hard to make an object invisible from every angle.
Making moving objects invisible is also tough. More
work is needed to develop useful invisibility. Many
physicists are trying to solve this and other problems.

The branch of physics known as optics deals with the behavior of light.

What Is Physics?

Physics is the study of how things move and interact. This includes huge things, like stars, and tiny things, like atoms. It also includes light and sound.

Discoveries in physics are made using experiments and measurements. Scientists use math and statistics to study the evidence they gather. With these results, they can describe the physical laws of our universe. Motions and interactions can be precisely described and even predicted using these laws. Sometimes, new discoveries lead to changes in these laws.

Physicists are scientists who study physics. Their work touches many fields. They are involved in medicine, climate science, and engineering.

Optics

The physics of light is known as optics. Scientists working on invisibility need to understand optics. People in this field may create lenses for telescopes or cameras. Optical scientists may also work with lasers or microscopes. The scientists study how light interacts with the rest of the universe.

One physicist may help with bank security. Another might study the planets. Physicists helped develop computers, making our modern world possible. Physics is in the world around us, and its possibilities seem endless.

Inventor Benjamin Franklin worked in the 1700s. In his autobiography, he wondered about future advances in science:

> *The rapid progress true science now makes, occasions my regretting sometimes that I was born so soon. It is impossible to imagine the height to which may be carried, in a thousand years, the power of man over matter. We may perhaps learn to deprive large masses of their gravity, and give them absolute levity, for the sake of easy transport. Agriculture may diminish its labor and double its produce; all diseases may by sure means be prevented or cured, not excepting even that of old age, and our lives lengthened at pleasure even beyond the antediluvian standard. O that moral science were in as fair a way of improvement, that men would cease to be wolves to one another, and that human beings would at length learn what they now improperly call humanity!*

Source: "Volume 31." The Papers of Benjamin Franklin. *The Packard Humanities Institute*, n.d. Web. Accessed June 24, 2015.

What's the Big Idea?

Read the text carefully. What is the main idea? What details does Franklin use to support this point? Have any of Franklin's predictions come true?

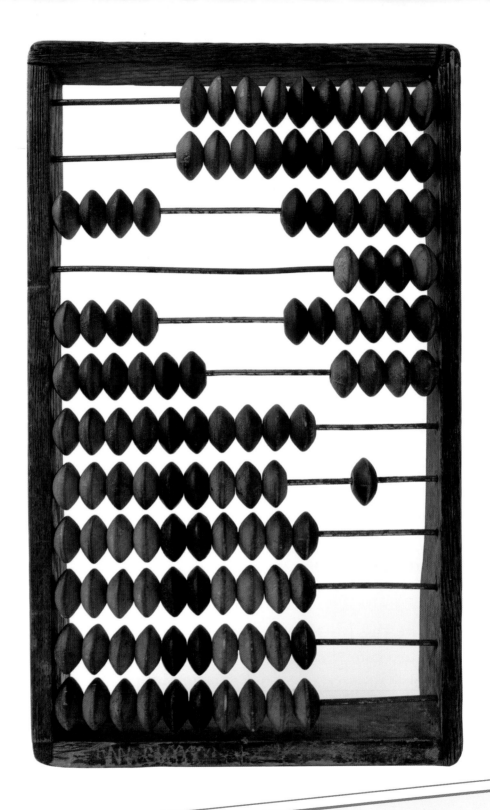

CHAPTER TWO

A SCIENCE AS OLD AS CIVILIZATION

Physics has been around for thousands of years. It has deep connections to math. Early mathematicians can be seen as the earliest physicists. By 2300 BCE, ancient Sumerians had created the abacus. This device was used for counting and math. Many ancient cultures developed math to describe the natural world.

Ancient people used the abacus for addition and subtraction.

The early Greek philosopher Aristotle lived in the 300s BCE. He described theories of how the world works. He thought rocks would always fall back to Earth when dropped. He believed this was because Earth and the rock were made of the same material. Aristotle also thought that heavy objects would fall faster than lighter ones. He was among the first thinkers to explore why and how things fall to the ground.

Physics Grows Up

In the 1500s, people challenged ancient beliefs. One famous experiment disproved the idea that heavy objects fall faster than light ones.

Aristotle's Physics

Aristotle wasn't just interested in how things worked on Earth. He was also curious about space. He believed different physical laws applied in space. On Earth, there was chaos. Earthquakes rattled and volcanoes erupted. But in space, nothing seemed to change. Many centuries later, Isaac Newton's work with gravity brought space and Earth together. He showed that everything follows the same physical rules.

Galileo was also an important astronomer. He discovered four of Jupiter's moons.

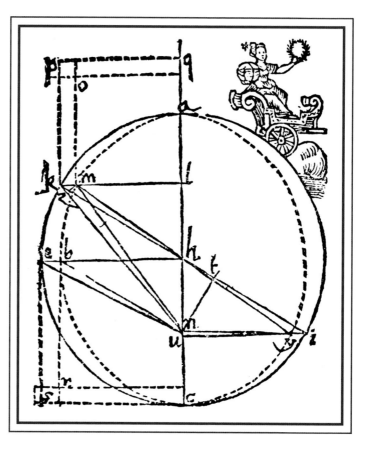

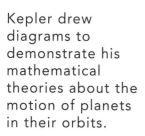

Kepler drew diagrams to demonstrate his mathematical theories about the motion of planets in their orbits.

Galileo Galilei was an Italian scientist. From the top of a tower he dropped objects of different weights. He recorded how long it took for the objects to hit the ground. The heavier objects hit the ground first, but only by a small amount. Galileo guessed that air resistance slowed the lighter objects. He believed that without air, all objects would fall at the same speed.

Galileo's experiment was an important event. It showed Aristotle's beliefs were wrong. Other scientists began doing experiments. They studied whether other ancient ideas were also incorrect. In the process, they made amazing new discoveries.

One place they looked was space. The movement of the planets was a hot topic of debate. In the early 1600s, most people believed planets moved in perfect circles. Then Johannes Kepler published his theories. He showed their orbits are actually elliptical. Isaac Newton later worked out the math behind gravity. He showed that it works the same way on Earth and in space.

Scientists were also solving mysteries on Earth. In the mid-1700s, Benjamin Franklin experimented with electricity. Physicists learned how electricity could be stored and used. By the late 1800s, power plants were lighting up cities.

Hubble's work broadened our understanding of the universe.

Modern Physics

In the 1900s, physicists studied the largest and smallest things in existence. Edwin Hubble used physics to discover that the universe was expanding. Other physicists were looking at atoms. Atoms are the building blocks of matter. They were considered the smallest objects. But physicists discovered they are made up of even smaller pieces. Atoms contained tiny particles such as electrons, protons, and neutrons. Physicists who studied these tiny

IN THE REAL WORLD

Atomic Bombs

In the early 1900s, physicists realized atoms could be split apart. This would release huge amounts of energy. The energy could even be used in a bomb. The United States sought to develop an atomic bomb during World War II (1939–1945). It wanted to build one before its enemies, Japan and Germany, did. On July 16, 1945, the first atomic bomb was tested in New Mexico. It left a huge crater. The blast was visible more than 200 miles (320 km) away. That August the US military dropped bombs on two Japanese cities. The bombs killed more than 100,000 people. The war ended weeks later when Japan surrendered.

Einstein is history's most famous physicist.

particles formed a new field of study. They called it quantum mechanics. Scientists built machines to smash atoms together. This revealed the smaller particles within. Quantum mechanics led to the development of computers, nuclear energy, and many other innovations.

There have been several famous physicists in recent history. In the early 1900s, Marie Curie made

discoveries about radiation. In 1915, Albert Einstein developed the theory of general relativity. This theory describes gravity's effects on space and time. In the 1970s, Stephen Hawking studied black holes. These are objects in space with very strong gravity. Even light cannot escape their pull. Today physicists continue investigating these and many other topics.

EXPLORE ONLINE

Chapter Two discusses gravity and orbits. Visit the website below to test these things for yourself. How do the results change when you increase an object's mass? What happens when more than two objects are involved? What can you learn about gravity from this website?

Gravity Simulator
mycorelibrary.com/physics

CHAPTER THREE

CAREERS IN PHYSICS

Most physicists belong to one of two main groups. Experimental physicists do hands-on experiments. Theoretical physicists work with computer simulations. Both types of physicists have a wide variety of careers available to them. Most work for universities, companies, or the government.

Modern experimental physicists often use complex, expensive equipment.

Academic Lab Physicists

When people think of scientists, they often think of white lab coats. It is true that many physicists work in laboratories. These labs are often found at universities. Scientists there often teach classes in addition to doing research.

In the lab, many scientists work on what is known as basic science. In this case, "basic" does not mean easy! Basic science involves the central facts of physics. Scientists study how atoms behave and interact. For example, much of the research done at the Large Hadron Collider (LHC) is basic science. The LHC is a particle accelerator in Europe. Inside its 16-mile (27-km) tunnel, particles are sent racing at one another. When they collide, the crash can produce the particles that make up atoms. The particles may exist for only a fraction of a second before they disappear.

Studying these particles helps scientists learn the basic principles of physics. These discoveries might not be useful right away. But they can help

The LHC uses huge magnets to accelerate tiny particles to high speeds.

us understand how the universe works.

Basic science can lead to applied science. This involves using science in the real world. Biophysicists do applied science. They study the physics of biology. They help create treatments for diseases such as cancer. Another field of applied physics is geophysics. Geophysicists may study earthquakes or other disasters. They can save lives by predicting and preparing for disasters.

Industry Physicists

Industry physicists work for private companies. They tend to focus on applied science that can be used to make products. Carmakers and energy corporations employ physicists. They may also work for small companies focused on specific parts of physics. A biophysicist might work for a company making artificial hearts.

Physics overlaps with other fields, especially engineering. An example of this can be seen in the development of new solar panels. These devices convert sunlight into electricity. Physicists identify the best materials for the panels. Then engineers can design and build them.

The divide between the work of academic and industry physicists can be

IN THE REAL WORLD
Energy Physicists

Solar power is not the only energy source physicists are studying. Some work with wind energy. Others find ways to get energy from ocean currents. Physicists also determine which energy sources are best for which regions. Places with lots of sunshine may work better for solar power. Windy areas may benefit from wind turbines. Physicists also study how to store and use energy. They work on improving battery technology. They learn how to make existing products more efficient so they do not need as much energy to function.

Solar panels are a major area of research for industry and academic physicists.

blurry. Both work with colleagues. Both seek funding and do research. One big difference is in their working environment. Academic physicists often teach and advise students. Physicists in industry may lead teams of other researchers. They may need to plan how to spend a limited research budget.

Government Physicists

Physicists also find careers in the government. Some work for departments such as the Department of Energy. These scientists often do work similar to that done by other physicists. They may study earthquakes or new energy sources. But there are some unique positions available for government physicists.

One department that offers unusual careers is the National Institute of Standards and Technology (NIST). NIST physicists create standard measurements. They use atomic clocks to keep precise time. They define the exact weight of a kilogram. Their work allows other physicists to get consistent results.

The National Aeronautics and Space Administration (NASA) employs many physicists. Some study Earth. They use satellites to observe the climate. Other NASA physicists study planets and stars. They use telescopes to observe these objects.

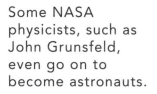

Some NASA physicists, such as John Grunsfeld, even go on to become astronauts.

Most data collected by government scientists is freely available. All physicists can use it. The general public can also see it if they wish.

In an article for the American Physical Society, medical physicist Albin Gonzalez talks about careers in physics and gives advice to students:

> Albin stresses the fact that you don't have to become a professor or researcher if you go into physics. "There are some very interesting jobs out there," he says. "The sky's the limit in terms of what you can do: you could be at a university or in a national laboratory dealing with huge projects, working in industry, power plants, hospitals, financial institutions or even setting up your own business."
>
> The best advice Albin has for students is simple: don't waste time! "Find out what moves you, what is exciting to you, what will make you happy every day that you go to work. And then set your goals, one little step at a time. Don't let anybody or anything tell you that you cannot do it," he says.

Source: "Albin Gonzalez." Careers in Physics. *American Physical Society,* 2015. Web. Accessed June 25, 2015.

Back It Up

Gonzalez uses evidence to support a point. Write a paragraph describing his point and listing the evidence he uses. Does Chapter Three contain additional evidence for or against this point?

THE FUTURE OF PHYSICS

The future of physics seems limitless. Today's research will result in amazing advances. Work in physics will lead to faster computers. It will bring us worlds of virtual reality. It will improve our understanding of the universe.

Quantum mechanics, which involves the motions and interactions of tiny subatomic particles, is a major area of study in modern physics.

Research on quantum computing may unlock new possibilities in computer technology.

Quantum Computing

One area of physics that will change the world is quantum mechanics. Quantum computing is an especially interesting field. Today's computers work using transistors. These are tiny pieces of metal that conduct electricity. Computers use millions of transistors to process information.

Researchers are developing new quantum computers. These machines use the behavior of subatomic particles to work. Scientists can build these computers smaller and faster than those we have today.

IN THE REAL WORLD

Creating Faster and Smarter Computers

How do you make a smarter computer? This is one challenge that quantum computing hopes to address. NASA researchers are trying to create a computer that can work much faster than a traditional computer. Such a computer might tackle problems that are too big for today's computers. One job would be to process the huge amount of data created by particle colliders.

First, physicists will need to learn how to control the behavior of such tiny particles.

Virtual Worlds

Physics will also make virtual reality possible in the future. You could put on a headset and feel as though you are in another place. Turning your head would also change your view in the virtual reality world. Video games, military training, and many other things could benefit from this technology.

However, virtual reality has faced one key problem. It can make people sick. The image can lag behind the user's head movements. When you turn your head, it takes the virtual world a moment to

Physics research has played a key role in making virtual reality possible.

The scientists at the LHC are expanding our knowledge of physics.

catch up. That lag is enough to make many people sick.

Physicists are working to overcome this issue. Part of the solution uses the science of optics. Light and lenses can trick the brain into thinking it is seeing the real world. Physicists alter the light from the headset to provide a realistic view. This helps users feel as though they are really in the virtual world.

More Collisions

Physics is also working to better understand our universe. The LHC is a great example of this. LHC physicists are looking for special particles. One of these is the Higgs boson. It is named for physicist Peter Higgs. A boson is a subatomic particle, like a proton or neutron. This particle could help explain how physics and the universe work.

Particle physicists work with a system known as the standard model. This model describes the relationships between particles and forces. It is the underlying theory behind physics. But for the standard

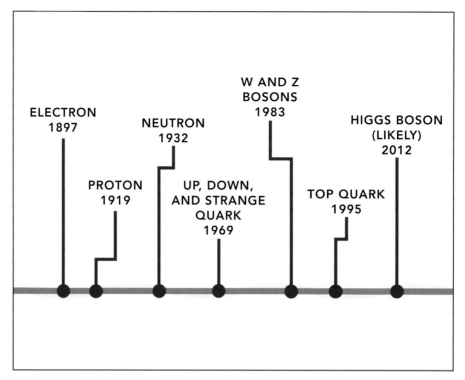

Timeline of Particle Discovery

In 1897, the electron was the first subatomic particle discovered. Since then, science has been on the hunt for more. The timeline above shows when several other major subatomic particles were discovered. How does the timeline help you better understand the development of quantum mechanics?

model to work, scientists predict the Higgs boson must exist. The LHC was built to find this particle. If it is found, it would provide evidence that the standard model is correct.

By 2015, data from the LHC suggested the Higgs boson might have been found. More work was needed to confirm these results. Physicists working on basic science continue to search for more particles.

Major advances have been made throughout the history of physics. From Newton to the Higgs boson, physicists have worked at the limit of human knowledge. The physicists of tomorrow will make discoveries that will push us even further. They will continue unlocking the secrets of the universe.

FURTHER EVIDENCE

Chapter Four suggests physics will be responsible for many changes in future technology. What was one of the main points of this chapter? What evidence is included to support this point? Find a quote from the website that supports the chapter's main point.

Physics of the Future
mycorelibrary.com/physics

- Physics studies all aspects of the world, both big and small.

- Physics is a discipline that crosses over into many others, such as medicine, geology, and astronomy.

- Physicists can be found in many different career locations, from academic settings to industry to the government.

- There are jobs in physics for those who want to work on purely mathematical and theoretical projects, such as creating theories about how the universe formed.

- There are jobs in physics for those who want to do experimental work, such as smashing atoms, building microscopes, or using telescopes to explore the stars.

- There will be even more demand in the future for physicists who can tackle the complex world of quantum mechanics, which might change how we interact with technology.

Why Do I Care?

Maybe physics isn't all that interesting to you. But that does not mean physics has no effect on your world. Write about three things you learned that showed you how physics has a positive influence in the world. Where do you see physics making a difference in your everyday life?

Take a Stand

The Large Hadron Collider originally cost about $4.75 billion to build. With the cost of experiments and additional building funds, it is estimated that it may cost about $13.25 billion to find the Higgs boson. This funding comes from government resources. Is the cost worth it? Write an argument for or against the cost to find the Higgs boson.

Surprise Me

Chapter Two talked about the history of physics. What two or three things surprised you about how people used to see the world? Why did you find those things surprising?

Tell the Tale

In Chapter One, you learned about invisibility technology. Imagine you have the technology to make any object invisible. Write a 200-word story talking about what you would make invisible and why.

GLOSSARY

abacus
an ancient device used for counting and mathematics

matter
the substances that make up the physical world

acoustic
relating to the sense of hearing

nuclear
relating to the nucleus of atoms

electricity
energy associated with the movement of charged particles, such as electrons

particle
a very small piece of matter, such as an electron or a proton

elliptical orbit
an oval-shaped path an object in space takes around another object

quarks
subatomic particles that make up protons, neutrons, and other types of particles

LEARN MORE

Books

Adams, Tom. *Feel the Force!* Somerville, MA: Templar Books, 2011.

Green, Dan. *Physics: Why Matter Matters!* New York: Kingfisher, 2008.

Westphal, Laurie E. *Hands-On Physical Science.* Waco, TX: Prufrock Press, 2008.

Websites

To learn more about STEM in the Real World, visit **booklinks.abdopublishing.com.** These links are routinely monitored and updated to provide the most current information available.

Visit **mycorelibrary.com** for free additional tools for teachers and students.

INDEX

ABOUT THE AUTHOR

Meg Marquardt has a bachelor's degree in physics and a master's degree in science journalism. She lives in Omaha, Nebraska, with her two science-minded cats, Lagrange and Doppler.